The Inner Child Workbook

Recovering your Inner Child   le

Autho

Copyright 2019

ISBN 9781692696634

Publisher/Impressum:

International Books

Christian Buß
Krementzstr. 9
50931 Cologne, Germany

Table of Contents

4

Introduction

Julie Perkins

North Carolina, Dec 1993

It was one of those snowy days in Raleigh, North Carolina, when almost everyone in the neighborhood was safe indoors except Julie's mom, Catherine. Typical of North Carolina, winter had come earlier than usual, this time about a week ahead of the neighboring states, but the harsh weather wasn't enough to sever Catherine from her grueling jobs. If she wasn't delivering pizza, she was stocking groceries at a supermarket or babysitting kids whose parents were out on a date, among others. After serving five years at the North Carolina Correctional Institution for Women, Catherine had failed to secure a suitable job that could afford her enough time for her eleven-year-old Julie. Instead, she had settled for meager jobs that paid by the hour and kept her away all day. Although the jobs could hardly pay her bills and sustain herself and Julie, Catherine kept on working, resolved never to return to drug peddling, which had kept her locked behind bars for so long. As a result, Julie was forced to spend most of the weekdays at her Granny's with her older cousins, Tommy, Arthur, and Whitney, whom she hardly got along with. On some weekends, when she wasn't with the large family, she was alone in Catherine's two-bedroom flat, sprawled on the floor or on the only sofa in the sitting room watching TV and half-hoping that Catherine would arrive before she slept off. Over time, her wishes withered into resigned acceptance that her mom was never meant to be there for her.

On this very night, while Julie was seeing *Blossom,* her favorite TV show, Nick, Catherine's latest boyfriend, staggered into the apartment, cold and heavily drunk. It wasn't unusual for Nick to spend the night at Catherine's even when she wasn't home, neither was it unusual for him to come in drunk, but on this occasion, he was so doused in cheap liquor that one could smell it all over him from a mile away. Nick could hardly stand erect, and Julie had to help him to the bedroom he shared with Catherine. He fell asleep just as soon as he hit the bed with his stinking coat and shoes still intact. Julie returned to her sitcom and soon fell asleep on the sofa.

Three hours later, woken by the discomfort arising from his shoes, Nick grudgingly lifted himself to pull them off. He also stripped off his coat and pants, and, barely conscious, made for the sitting room to grab a drink from the small bar. He had taken two swigs when his eyes settled on Julie's tender chocolate-colored laps, which were given away by her undone pajamas. Without as much as a second thought, Nick reached for them and was soon grazing his palm upwards when Julie started from her sleep. Nick responded by pressing his weight on her, but she was slick enough to reach for the ceramic mug from which she drank her milk some hours earlier, which was lying a few yards away. She gripped it hard and hit the base on Nick's left temple. Instantly, he lost consciousness and collapsed on her. She was surprised by her own composure and breathed a sigh of relief before heaving the wasted and unconscious Nick off herself. Luckily, he did not bleed. She dragged him back to the bedroom and locked the door from outside, ran into her room and bolted the door. She hoped it wasn't real.

The following morning, Julie was shocked that Nick never acted like he tried to force himself on her. Her shock grew into confusion when she began to entertain doubts on the events of the night. Could she have dreamed it all? A few days later, Julie summoned the courage to tell Catherine and instantly regretted it. Catherine did not only misunderstand the situation but also smacked her in the face for 'cooking up lies'!

San Jose, July 2015

'I beg to differ, Mr chairman!', started Jeremy Morgan, a member of the executive board of Global Travels.

I'm afraid we cannot promote Miss Perkins to the position of the Head of Human Resource department just yet', he continued rather bluntly. *'Prejudice apart, the lady is admittedly intelligent but does not possess the will and self-control needed to run the department. We speak of a lady who cannot sufficiently air her opinions, let alone sell them to others. We had better reconsider that decision for the benefit of this organization',* he concluded, settling back in his chair.

When Julie Perkins received news that she would not be made the H.O.D of Human Resource despite being the most favorite for the post, she was sad but not exactly disappointed. It wasn't the first time she had been denied privileges on account of her inability to express herself and control her emotions. Since she ran away from her mother some twenty-two years ago, her life has been heavily influenced by the ugly events from back then. As if her failure in career wasn't enough, she could hardly maintain a romantic relationship. The men always left, however hard she tried to keep them! As a result, she grew bitter, lonely and dejected.

*****

It is true that our adult lives and personalities are largely influenced by our childhood experiences. That we often neglect this fact or fail to accept it does not make it any less of a truth. As a matter of fact, going by the outcome of a 2016 America Psychology Study, one in every three persons worldwide is adversely affected by some events in their past. As we go through life, moving from one developmental stage to another in terms of biological development, social responsibilities, family, and career, among others, we take with us certain influences of the past stages. In other words, the impacts taken from previous stages form key components of the new ones. This implies that, like Julie Perkins, if one's formative stage is replete with situations that make them bitter, they will inevitably grow up to become sad persons, or if they were forced to conceal their true expressions during their childhood days, they will certainly find it difficult, if not literally impossible, to air their personal views later in life.

On the positive side, even though life is not exactly a bed of roses, there are many good experiences from childhood such as adequate parental care, a well-to-do socioeconomic background, social acceptance from family and friends, and so on, which positively influence an individual's outlook toward life in their later stages. Whether positive or otherwise, every individual has an impressionable version of themselves especially at childhood, which, however influenced, affects one's growth and adult personality. This version is better put as *the inner child* or *the inner self*. As negative impacts are more likely to have far-reaching consequences, it becomes a necessity to minimize the adverse events and experiences to which individuals are exposed during childhood. However, we must admit that this is easier said than done, because of the multifarious family backgrounds and upbringing. The good news is that irrespective of your childhood experiences and the impacts your inner child has on your adult life, you can take matters in your own hands by healing your inner child of all negative imprints. Yes, it is possible!

It is my belief that, with this book in your hand, you are looking to recover your inner child and heal it of all negative impacts. You are already one step in the right direction. In this book, I set out to resolve all your worries about healing your inner child. You will discover your inner child archetype, how to identify a wounded inner child, a trusted guide to lead you through the healing process, and ultimately realize how you can reconnect with your inner child for a fulfilling adult life. Brace up for a ride back in time into the mysteries of the inner child.

THE INNER CHILD

What it is; What it is not

In every real man, a child is hidden that wants to play.

Friedrich Nietzsche

Is the Inner Child Real?

I have been confronted with tons of questions bordering around the reality of the inner child, especially from friends and individuals who have at one time or the other read my contents on the subject. Many have questioned the truism behind the concept of the inner child, given the fact that as humans develop, we tend to outgrow our childhood interests, behaviors, and desires. This position is, of course, logical, but what it fails to put into consideration is the fact that despite these visible changes, there are traces of the childhood personality left in us, which influence a large part of who we are as adults. Against this backdrop, I make an attempt to explain in concise paragraphs what the inner child truly means.

The inner child does not necessarily imply that there is a child living within us, or that everyone is a child or behaves childishly, but refers to the loving gentle childlike aspect of every individual. Also known as the child within, the wonder child or the wounded child, a person's inner child comprises all the learnings acquired, experiences underwent, events and situations witnessed, emotions exposed to, as well as care received by an individual during the formative childhood stage, especially before puberty. Every individual passes through this highly impressionable stage at which everything that happens around us or directly to us contributes maximally to our beliefs, prejudices, interests, dislikes and overall personality even though we hardly notice this. It is often the case that we might have forgotten most of these childhood events and situations, but whether we have or not, the impact they have on our psychology remains ever intact. I'll tell you a quick story to illustrate this; sometime within the age of 4 and 5 back in elementary school, we were taught a rhyme which read thus:

Standard living

Standard living

I am a teacher in my country

Due to my growing speech abilities, I, as well as many other kids my age then, would mispronounce *Standard living* as *Sandalili,* which of course is meaningless but added melody to the song. On and on that way, I continued to mispronounce the words and fell in love with my own version so much that even as I grew older to realize that it ought to be called *Standard Living,* I preferred to call it my own way.

Now, this might be a rather comic and perhaps too simple way to describe the significance of the inner child but it is sufficient to set us off on the right foot. I should mention that most times, the events and situations that contribute to the inner child personality are often orchestrated by others around, especially the significant people who wield so much influence on our upbringing, such as our parents, siblings, teachers, and religious leaders, among others.

In other words, we are not often passive contributors to our inner child. Consider our friend, Julie Perkins. Her inability to emphasize her will later in life was primarily caused by the fact that she had no one to discuss intimate issues with as a child, and when she ever made to express herself, she was cowered into silence by people who should have encouraged her to speak on. As a result, her inner child was wired to believe in bottling up emotions!

Origin

Before I dwell on whether the inner child is a mere myth or is backed by science, I provide a brief historical backup to establish its essence and significance.

Swiss psychiatrist and psychoanalyst Carl Gustav Jung (1875 - 1961) has been credited with founding the concept of the inner child even though several other scholars expounded it differently.

Carl Gustav Jung (1875 - 1961)

He mentioned the Child archetype as one of the archetypes that contribute to the development of the self. According to Jung, the Child archetype serves as a way of connecting to the past and for recollecting all our childhood stage experiences. He adds that a clear understanding of who we were as children will help to determine who we want to be in the future.

In addition to Carl's child archetype theory, several scholars have built on the inner child concept. Charles Whitfield, for example, called it 'The child within' in his 1987 book titled *Healing the Child Within: Discovery and Recovery of Adult Children for Dysfunctional Families* in which he dwells on the need to discover one's inner child and recover it if wounded. More significantly, Lucia Capacchione propounded a trusted method of healing the inner child via what she termed an art therapy that involves re-parenting the inner child.

Although her view of the inner child was limited to an individual's emotional, creative, spiritual and psychological needs, the healing techniques suggested in her 1991 book titled *Recovery of your Inner Child* have grown in acceptance worldwide over time. More so, her view on nurturing the adult despite having passed the childhood stage still gains relevance in the inner child scholarship till date.

If we may now go back to the question on the inner child — real or not —, the inner child is obviously a psychological reality that plays a significant role in human development. Buried in the subconscious mind of an individual, the inner child affects our thought process, reactions to situations around, decision making, and virtually every key domain of our lives. Although we fail to acknowledge it, all our behaviors, both positive and otherwise, are influenced by our inner child. It, therefore, goes without mention that a wounded inner child will result in negative or destructive behavioral patterns, as exemplified by Julie Perkins. Mind you, that is just one situation out of millions worldwide. Most terrorists, for example, have been found to lack proper parental care and love during childhood, and in the same vein, certain individuals who find it difficult to enter into or maintain healthy romantic relationships are largely likely victims of homes with domestic violence.

Most times, we cannot help the outcomes of our inner child personality except through conscious therapy, which might involve accentuating the positive sides of the inner child and addressing the negative sides.

The inability to effectively manage one's inner child makes one a mere adult child. Psychologically, one is not an adult by chronological age. Adulthood in this context depends on your ability to identify, acknowledge and accept your inner child as it is, and thereafter parent it properly. This is necessary because the inner child has both the good and the bad sides to it. It is recommendable, as part of the healing process, to revive and adopt the childlike qualities such as happiness, contentment, playfulness, innocence, peaceful cooperation with others, trust, love, and so on. This is a core necessity because, during the growing process, these positive qualities are stifled by life situations. On the other hand, however, the inner child could also embody negative feelings which it needs to be rid of. Such negative feelings include hurt, disappointment, betrayal, anger, trauma, fear, and insecurity, among others. Whereas many people think that they have outgrown their childhood negative feelings, they fail to acknowledge the fact that such feelings only lurk somewhere within, and subtly manifests in their adult lives. Until you are willing to completely purge yourself of all negative childhood feelings, I'm afraid you will continue to live under the shadows!

Is the Inner Child So Important?

The most potent muse of all is our own inner child.

Stephen Nachmanovitch

Having established the facts behind the inner child, it is pertinent to touch on its necessity to humanity. If, as a grown-up, you have ever envied children their unalloyed peace with themselves and others, their worry-free life and their complete disregard for the future or the past, you would value the inner child within you. Although our adult lives largely steal away the innocence and bliss that comes with childhood, from time to time, we reconnect to the childhood world and feel the childlike experience again. At such times, the feeling is indescribable. Yet, that is just one of the ways the inner child helps you to find and reconnect to yourself. In addition to this, the inner child helps you achieve the following:

➤ **Increased creativity**

Creativity represents a miraculous coming together of the uninhibited energy of the child.

Norman Podhoretz

Creativity flows much easier when we explore our innate abilities, consciously or otherwise, without entertaining the fear of being castigated or mocked for errors. This is exactly what children enjoy that allows them enough room to conjure up new beautiful images, for example. Reconnecting with your inner child, therefore, allows you to think up ideas without being held down by the usual adult chains of self-doubt and fear of not being appreciated. Each time you come up with an entirely novel idea or invention, you tap into the reserve of your inner child confidence, without which you would fail to think up anything new or creative for fear of being mocked or solely because of doubts in your own abilities. How many times have you picked up a pen to write down a few lines of poetry, but almost immediately dropped it because you thought it would be a mess of a poem, or because you feel poetry is not exactly your thing? The same applies to your business ideas, scientific inventions, diplomatic tactics, etc. You would need to reconnect with your inner child to gain the confidence required to pull through a creative exercise.

➢ **Discovering and Unleashing your Repressed Emotions**

So, like a forgotten fire, a childhood can always flare up again within us.

Gaston Bachelard

Reaching into your inner child enables you to find the causes of your adult problems. Most, if not all, of the challenges we face as adults stem from, or at least are aided by, our reactions to situations because of the emotions long bottled within us. These emotions hold you from breaking new grounds, making new discoveries, expressing yourself in your social circles, and breaking free from the constraints that hold you back. By reconnecting to your inner child, you are gradually set free from adult troubles caused by such emotions. From another perspective, reaching in helps you to identify the negative emotions trapped within as a result of your childhood experiences. Identifying them is the first step in unleashing them. Pent-up feelings are capable of limiting us. You may compare the situation to an athlete who has bags of sand tied to his feet. You can't go as far and as fast as you ought to until you unleash it!

➢ **Resolving Harmful Behavioral Patterns**

I believe that this neglected, wounded, inner child of the past is the major source of human misery.

Bradshaw sums it all up in this beautiful quote. Our lives would literally be free of troubles if we all had an all-positive inner child, but hard as we wish, this is never the case. First off, neglecting our inner child is a major cause of the challenges we are confronted with. Having abandoned the inner child, we fail to recognize that most of our adverse behaviors that instigate difficulties are consequences of the negative emotions from our childhood. In order to address this, it is important to go back to the source. Having identified the causal factors, we can then address the problems adequately. Considering Julie Perkins as our case study again, in order to fully address her inability to sustain a healthy romantic relationship, the behavior must first be traced to the situations that imprinted it on her inner child. In another view, embracing positive childlike traits such as warmth, unconditional love, trust, and self-confidence, among many others will help you jettison your harmful manners.

> **Increased Self-care, Self-consciousness and Self-value**

Love yourself every day, even as your skin wrinkles and your bones ache.

Anonymous

Paying attention to your inner child inevitably makes you conscious of yourself, thereby increasing your understanding of your true desires, interests, fears and how to overpower them, your strengths, creative abilities, skills and all that make you a unique individual. This way, you get to value yourself for who you truly are, and avoid unnecessary comparison with others. More so, you become fully aware of the causes of your own behavioral patterns, as well as what to do to address negative behaviors. The inner child also helps you to realize your preferences in certain situations and to identify what precisely works for you in a world of teeming options. With a full realization of your inner self comes the natural desire to nurture, parent it well and keep it ageless because you understand that a larger part of your adult life depends on your inner child. In the words of Mencius, *the great man is he who does not lose his child's heart.*

INNER CHILD ARCHETYPES

What Kind of Inner Child is yours?

The shoe that fits one person pinches another; there is no recipe for living that suits all cases.

Carl Jung

In the journey to recover your inner child, it is necessary to identify what archetype of the inner child is yours. This is especially important to help you tailor your recovery energy properly. It is a common mistake to think that what works for a friend, mentor, colleague, siblings or even one's parents will work for you. This is far from the reality as far as the inner child is concerned. Every living being possesses a set of distinct experiences, desires, and so on, that make their inner child unique. It doesn't matter whether you were raised by the same parents, or brought up in the same environment at the same time, or you are of the same age, or attended the same elementary school or share the same interests as others. Your inner child will definitely be different from theirs. It is against this backdrop that you must understand that you need to address your inner child as an individual entity separate from those of others.

Despite the individuation, however, Carl Jung broadly classifies the human inner child archetypes into six distinct groups. It is my belief that as we launch into the six archetypes in the subsequent paragraphs of this chapter, you will find the group to which your inner child belongs, and that this will be a bold step in identifying how to heal and recover it. More so, an understanding of your inner child archetype, and by extension both its positive and negative components, helps you to identify better with it as part of your core personality, and as a result, you can harness it positively. The six inner child archetypes are discussed as follows:

The Orphan Child Archetype

Some scholars prefer to call this archetype the abandoned child archetype. It is found in individuals who tend to view themselves as independent beings even at the early stage of their lives when they ought to be under parental care and guidance. It is caused mainly by feelings of loneliness, rejection, abandonment, lack of care, etc. Note that having an orphan child archetype does not necessarily mean that one is an orphan. More often than not, it is the feeling, as the name suggests, that one does not enjoy adequate parental attention and love. Children raised by parents who were too busy with work to create time for their kids often possess this inner child archetype. On the other hand, the situation could be literal, in which children who were orphaned very early in life, and as a result received little or no parental care during their childhood days are conditioned to believe that they are not meant to be loved. Individuals with this archetype are always too reserved, feel isolated and constantly shut others out of their emotions. They also avoid large groups and are almost always alone, if not lonely. On the positive end, however, individuals with the orphan child archetype are quick to develop survival instincts and other life skills, take responsibility for themselves and are generally independent. When the inner child is well harnessed, they are able to make decisions for themselves, overcome their fears with little or no help from others.

The Wounded Child Archetype

Also known as the injured child, this archetype is typical of people who have experienced a lot of pain and abuse, either physical or emotional, during their formative age. Those who suffer repression and sexual abuse also fall into this category. Such abuses might have been inflicted on them by bullies at school, teachers, and so on. It is worse when the abuse is a repeated one inflicted upon them by trusted family associates such as a sibling, relative or parent. Individuals with this inner child archetype hardly forget such traumatic experiences, and, worse still, it influences how they react to other people and to situations around them as they grow to become adults. They also become withdrawn and find it difficult to trust others. In chronic cases, they form stereotypic opinions of others and hardly let go of such opinions all through their lifetime. Such persons often become used to the abusive relationship and consider themselves no more valuable than mere objects meant to be used. They nurture hatred and blame their abusers for all their life failures. In very extreme cases, when they are pushed to the wall, their hatred could grow into unpremeditated deadly attacks on their predators. The positive side to this archetype, however, is that, if well recovered, they redirect their hatred toward care and love for others who are victims of the same situation. They are quick to forgive and show compassion to others with the same ugly experiences.

The Nature Child Archetype

If you know a person who loves nature so well, they might just have the nature child archetype. Individuals with this archetype are helplessly in love with natural things such as animals, plants, gardens, streams, and the environment at large. They prefer to stay in nature than among others because that is where they find the most comfort, and they enjoy a deep connection with it. They value the time spent in nature, and will not exchange it for anything. Sometimes, they presumably communicate with nature. The problem with this archetype is that the love for nature could be excessive, and could affect other aspects of their lives, especially their careers and relationship with others because they always prefer to stay alone in nature. They could also grow into extreme love for animals over humans! However, when this archetype is injured, they could become abusive to people and animals.

The Magical Child Archetype

According to Hugh Magnus MacLeod, everyone is born creative. However, quite unfortunately, not everyone grows up to become creative or to utilize their creativity. This is the inner child archetype that houses the childhood freedom to explore one's innate skills and abilities. The truth is that we don't grow up to become creative or invent ideas. On the contrary, it is as we grow up that we abandon our creative abilities and ideas, unused. The story is, however, a different one for individuals with the magical child archetype. They are those who were allowed ample freedom to explore during their childhood, and as an outcome, have seen the magical infiniteness in the world's possibilities. They believe that everything is possible, only that the right way has to be found. They are deep thinkers who believe in the power of the mind to think up ground-breaking ideas that can make the world a better place. They are often inquisitive, carefree and adventurous idealists. As beautiful as this inner child archetype sounds, it, notwithstanding, has its downside. Such persons could be drawn into their imagination so much that they lose track of reality, and instead live in the world of fiction, movies, and fairytale. They could also be dogmatic with their ideas, and fail to accept opinions of others especially when such opinions differ from theirs or are not idealistic. They could become pessimistic and unnecessarily drawn away from others. They are often recluses who live in their minds and in the world of ideas.

The Divine Child Archetype

Childhood is most associated with purity. It is believed that one is yet unspoiled by the blemishes of adulthood. This is exactly what the divine child archetype emphasizes. Adults with this inner child archetype possess childlike innocence, enviable character, pure heart, unadulterated love, and a good friendliness. Based on this, this archetype is believed to be most connected to the divine realm. People with this inner child archetype grow to become lovable individuals, and sometimes leaders, both in the secular and spiritual realms. They love unconditionally and respect people's opinions. They care a lot about those around them and put others first. The negative side attached to this archetype is that it could tilt towards pride and self-elevation due to its godlike characteristics. More so, such individuals could be overshadowed by negativities, thereby making them intolerant of others around, and their supposed ungodly ways of life. They could also find it extremely difficult to check their dislike for those who they consider lesser in rank and dignity than them.

The Eternal Child Archetype

This is the inner child that James Broughton refers to when he said *I'm happy to report that my inner child is still ageless.* For individuals with this inner child archetype, life is all rosy and easy peasy. They are the set of persons who received adequate, if not excessive, parental care during their childhood days. This class of individuals is hardly exposed to life difficulties, and as a result, they come to believe that life is smooth all-round. They are perpetually childlike in behavior, thinking and in reacting to situations. They are ageless in mind and in spirit, and always seek to have fun. More so, they are bent on remaining young and carefree. They do not allow themselves to be burdened by life responsibilities. Conversely, however, people with the eternal child archetype fail to take full charge of the responsibilities that come with adulthood. They become excessively dependent on others, especially their parents and siblings, and as a result become unreliable. They cannot be trusted with serious tasks at work or in the home. They would rather relinquish their roles to others. Taking on leadership roles at home, work or in social circles is extremely difficult for them, and most times, they find it difficult to take decisions of their own.

It is my belief that all along, you would have discovered which of these archetypes describes you the most. Although you might have found dots of your personality in three or more or perhaps all of them, you would have found one which relates to you almost perfectly. That is your child archetype. With the knowledge of the positives and negatives associated with your archetype, you can now assess yourself to see if you are in perfect alignment with it. Where this is not the case, which is most definitely not, the next stage is to begin to look out for ways to heal your inner child. This inevitably leads you to methods of recovering your inner child, which will be discussed later in this book.

Nine Signs to Look out for

When childhood dies, its corpses are called adults.

Brian Aldiss

Can we help having an injured, or worse still, dead inner child? Given that we all pass through life's developmental stages from childhood to adulthood, this is almost impossible. As we grow up, we are forced by time and nature to witness life-changing events and undergo impactful experiences, which may be positive or otherwise. Like the soles on a wet muddy path., these experiences leave us with significant indelible influences that shape our growth process over time. In the process, we gradually lose touch with our inner child.

Yet, this may be described as a rather simple natural way like the passing of time, via which we drift away from the inner child personality. This is a phenomenon that we cannot help. In the same vein, the inner child could be gravely wounded via specific untoward situations that occur to us by some external unnatural factors which are equally, if not more, dangerous. Examples of such situations include maltreatment, bullying, harassment of any sort, rape, repression, starvation, excessive pampering, accidents, neglect, and so on. By virtue of these circumstances, especially if they occur during one's formative period, an individual's inner child may be grossly injured. As it is the case that no individual ever enjoys a completely hitch-free childhood through adulthood, we are all definitely victims of a wounded inner child, but at various degrees.

Against this background, it becomes a core necessity for every human alive to heal and recover their inner child. The problem with this, however, is that tons of people worldwide cannot tell when their inner child has been injured, or which aspects of it precisely are affected. In the recovery process, you must be able to do this. At this point, it is to address this common deficiency that I provide the following signs to look out for. Bear in mind that the cues provided here are not ultimate on their own and are not universal to every individual, but then, they will serve as a guide through your individual inner child discovery.

> **Hiding your True Feelings**

I cannot understand what you do not say.

Kate McGahan

This is one of the most obvious signs exhibited by individuals with a wounded inner child. Given that they have been hurt, abused, repressed, bullied or harassed, as the case may be, they conceal their feelings and continue to bear the hurt. In the worst-case scenario, victims consider themselves absurd to be the ones suffering such situations, most definitely thinking that they are alone in it. How wrong! As a result, they prefer to keep their true feelings bottled within. This explains why they almost never share their pains with others, unknown to them that divulging one's hurt to others is a major step in the healing process. Most victims grow up with this inner child attitude and sometimes unfairly expect their partners to understand them as they are. Unfortunately, not everyone can understand your unspoken words. When they are coerced to, victims of a wounded inner child will prefer to alleviate their hurts and hide their true feelings so as not to look like the devil with the sore head. This situation permeates all their life domains including family and work. Apart from getting hurt the more, they often give the wrong impression to others.

➤ Failure to Trust or Believe in Others

We are not strangers. It's a lack of trust that keeps us separated.

Michael R. French

It is logical to expect that one of the most common consequences of an injured inner child is lack of trust. Most of the events that occur during childhood, leading to a wounded inner child are caused by close relations who we believe in — parents, siblings, friends, teachers, and so on. The very little, and sometimes serious, things they do to hurt us in the growing age dampen our trust in people. We begin to trust less and doubt more. When this is unchecked, we grow up with the same mindset that no one can be trusted. This mindset often leads to more serious situations such as negativity and makes it difficult for victims to share their problems with others. Individuals with trust problems are stereotypic in their opinions of others, and keep their problems to themselves.

➤ **Hiding or Overblowing your Ego**

Don't talk about yourself; it will be done when you leave.

Wilson Mizner

Ego describes your personal identity and sense of self-esteem. On a neutral level, ego isn't dangerous to your personality nor your relationship with others. However, a very small ego or an overblown one is, and this can be traced to your childhood experiences. When you think too little of yourself, and find yourself constantly apologizing for other people's wrongs, for example, it could be that your pride has been bashed by one childhood situation or the other. Such persons are prone to further abuse and domination even as adults. On the other hand, excessive ego is also a product of an injured inner child. Individuals with the eternal child archetype who were raised with the orientation that the world revolves around them, are mostly found in this category. They grow up to become disliked by others around because they are often haughty, bossy and disrespectful.

➤ Insecurity

Most bad behavior comes from insecurity.

Debra Winger

Do you often feel insecure around people? You should check your inner child. People who grew up in homes with domestic violence, or suffered child abuse in their childhood days are found to be victims of insecurity in their adult life. They become unsure of their own abilities, having been forced to believe that they are worthless. They also entertain fear of others, and would rather remain in recluse. However, when they can't help being among others, they make to hide their insecurities in haughtiness, jealousy, and spite. Insecurity may also stem from the feeling of being inefficient, or being completely useless. While growing, many children are put under the pressure of comparison by their parents or significant others. You have most probably heard your parents say statements such as *'Taylor already solves difficult sums, and you can't do nothing!' or 'Aby now babysits her twin siblings. All you do is play around.'* Even when these comparisons are not clearly spelled, they do as much mental damage to the child. It goes without mention that the victims see themselves to be inferior to those who they are compared to, and inevitably feel insecure around them.

➤ Loss of Confidence in Oneself and One's Abilities

It took me a long time not to judge myself through someone else's eyes.

Sally Field

Closely related to insecurity is loss of confidence. This is another sign of a wounded inner child you should look out for. Every negative comment passed by parents on their children, or every moment of comparison does more than discouraging them. Such children are forced to lose their intrinsic motivation, and depend heavily, if not solely, on assessments from others. They are the set of children who grow up to become dependent adults who do not only fail to make decisions on their own but also rely too much on others for approval of their actions. They feel inadequate and incapable, and therefore find it difficult to accept that they are independently capable of achieving Ife goals, but instead, put all their hopes in those around. Such individuals are quite prone to exploitation.

➢ Excessive Worry

Worry does not empty tomorrow of its sorrow, it empties today of its strength.

Corrie Ten Boom

For individuals whose childhood was replete with one catastrophic event after the other, nothing is good or fun about life. They hold the pessimistic belief that happiness is only temporal, and a nursery bed for a bigger bout of gloominess. They live their lives in perpetual fear that the next moment can only be worse. As a result, they lose the mental will and strength to fight difficulties when they arise. Adults with this inner child signal might be living just fine or doing pretty well in their career and other involvements, but that is not enough to stop them from thinking and believing that the worst is yet to come. Worry is a mental imprint that has long been stamped on their inner child by adverse events from their childhood. As a result, they feel completely powerless to fight it. If you show this sign, you might go as far as resigning to the fate that what will be will be. Your inner child has been brutally battered.

> **Inertia**

Even if you are on the right track, you'll get run over if you just sit there.

Will Rogers

Another sign you might notice if your inner child is injured is the stark unwillingness to get things rolling. This sign is related to the one previously discussed — worry. Because your inner child is injured, you inevitably dwell on the hurt of the past so much that it robs you of the energy to get past them and start a new course of life. Your little energy and resources are primarily spent on trying to suppress your feelings, and as a result, all your attention is drawn to it, unknown to you that the more you dwell in that situation, the more the pain resurfaces.

> ➢ **Excessive Self-Criticism**

We are never so much disposed to quarrel with others as when we are dissatisfied with ourselves.

William Hazlitt

Another most vital sign to look out for is self-criticism blown out of proportion. It is true that you should be your own biggest fan and at the same time your own strictest critic. However, this must be done with some moderation. Individuals with a wounded inner child are excessively harsh on themselves. This is often because they have been forced by the situations revolving around their childhood to accept that they are useless, and can achieve nothing. Those who give in to this deceit recede into self-criticism, constantly blaming themselves for their situation. On the other hand, those who direly wish to break free from their inner child jinx react differently. In reaction, they drive themselves a little too hard and also blame themselves for their failures. In very extreme cases, this grows into complete self-hatred.

➢ **Fear of Failure**

"When we give ourselves permission to fail, we, at the same time, give ourselves permission to excel."

Eloise Ristad

Are you scared of failure? That could just be your way of showing your injured inner child! There is literally nothing wrong with failing. In the words of Henry Ford, *failure is an opportunity to begin again, more intelligently.* People who fear to fail do so mainly because they have been heavily criticized for failing sometime during their impressionable age, or they have been wrongly made to believe that life is all about winning, and there is no room for failure. As motivational as this charge sounds, it is misguided. Such individuals never accept failure, and as a result, fear to fail. They drive themselves unnecessarily hard to avoid failure. This is evidently a manifestation of an injured inner child. Life can't be all rosy always. This realization will help you understand the workings of life better. The fear of failure is not necessarily a motivation for success, but a sign of a misguided inner child.

At this juncture, I must necessarily stress that the signs provided above are pivotal but not ultimate to assessing your inner child. Notwithstanding, if you check three or more of the signs, you may rest assured that your inner child requires a therapy. Having identified and acknowledged the signs you manifest, your next challenge should be what healing methods to apply to your injured inner child in order to break free from its negative shackles and enjoy the positive fun and creative side. The answers to your question are provided in the subsequent chapters of this book.

RECONNECTING WITH YOUR INNER CHILD

Childhood Roots of Adult Happiness

Man is most nearly himself when he achieves the seriousness of a child at play.

Heraclitus

So far in the journey of recovering your inner child, it is my belief that your mind has been opened into a world of discovery of the truths behind the inner child, that you have identified your inner child archetype, and also discovered the likely factors responsible for your wounded inner child. Based on the foregoing, healing work is necessary. A core part of the healing process is the point of reconnecting with your inner child. You must probably be curious to know why it is necessary to reconnect to one's inner child which presumably has disappeared into the abyss of time. Well, not exactly. Your inner child embodies all your abilities in their raw unadulterated form, your strengths yet unused, as well as your mind yet unspoiled by life. Simply put, your inner child is you in your best state. In order to enjoy a fulfilling adult life, therefore, you need this 'perfect' state.

It is important to meet and reconnect with your inner child. Do you wonder where it is? Right there within you! A reconnection would require you to keep in constant touch with it, care for it and nurture it properly on a daily basis. This might seem like an absurd thing to do because your inner child isn't with you in person, but you must realize that it is this belief that has led you to abandon it all along. Consider your inner child as a separate entity, and of course, an innocent child in need of all the care possible; care which can only be given it by you! Note that this isn't just about you or what you want, but what your inner child needs. In the rest of this chapter, I suggest very simple and practical ideas that you may adopt on a daily basis to help you re-parent, reconnect with, and give your inner child all the laughter, fun, attention, love, compassion and whatnot that you have hitherto deprived it. It is my belief that if you practice them well, you will find these ideas extremely useful and productive.

❖ Address yourself as a child

Nobody says harsh words to a child, right? That's the purpose! Rather than bug your mind with the schedule for the next day, your business engagements and plans for the next week, loans that need to be paid, family involvements, the growing bills, your demanding boss at work or your cheating partner, you should instead dwell on the little things that interest you such as games, stories and songs.

❖ Your inner child wants to be cooed and pampered

Sadly, nobody will do this for you as an adult. Tell yourself the sweet things your inner child wants to hear. Remind yourself how beautiful and cute you were as a child. Interact peacefully in solitude. Speak softly, patiently and with love. Remind yourself — and by extension your inner child — that you are loved just the way you are. You do not have to be anything or anyone else, and you don't have any business proving your worth to anyone. Pay extra attention to the seemingly little things that pertain to you alone, such as your birthday and your achievements. Be genuinely happy!

❖ Get a favorite spot for meeting with your inner child

If you can remember any of your most favorite spots as a child, it will go a long way to speed up the process. However, if the specific spots are no more available or accessible, a similar place would serve. Say, for example, a poolside, garden, an open field, etc, for meeting, talking and playing.

❖ Assure your inner child

Kids need an assurance of your attention to gain confidence, don't they? Give your inner child so much assurance. Assure him/her of your love, attention, and care. Admit that you've been in the wrong for abandoning him/her all the while, but that they can rest assured of your attention from now onwards. Tell him/her how much you love and respect them, and how much you are proud of them. Assure them of your protection, and that you will keep him/her safe from people who might have negative influences on them or hurt them. Assure him/her of freedom, and that they will never be forgotten again.

❖ Sing songs and play with your inner child

You know how much babies love melodious songs and how much they like to play. Your inner child wants that too. Remember your most favorite songs as a child, and sing them to yourself. Play with your inner child. Draw out little images and make carvings if that is your childhood thing. This is the hallmark of creativity.

❖ Keep your inner child away from toxic people

Here is one important point to note as you undergo this healing process. Failure to pay proper attention to this could sabotage the entire process. Remember that you are going through a delicate process of reconciling with your inner child. It will help to do away with people such as colleagues or superiors at work, partners in a romantic relationship, as well as events that will jeopardize your efforts.

Reconnecting with your inner child is a subtle process that requires much attention and care, and this can only be done by you. Remember that your inner child is the root of all the happiness and fulfillment you can enjoy as an adult. To deprive your inner child of his or her true nature is to mortgage your happiness. You must, therefore, take it as a core responsibility to ensure that the people and situations which forced your inner child into relegation are kept away from your consciousness even as an adult. You may choose to practice the ideas suggested above as many times as you deem fit, but it is highly recommendable to let your inner child decide the cycle.

THE INNER CHILD WORK

Exercises for Healing the Inner Child

The older we get, the more we need to heal our inner child.

Jay Shetty

Your inner child remains with you for a lifetime. Perhaps it would have been less demanding to nurture if it came only for a while, or on an occasional basis. Fortunately and unfortunately, this is not the case. Fortunately because, if visible and significant enough, the inner child contributes positively to your life, influencing your day-to-day development, and balances your life in its multiple dimensions — family, social, career, emotional and physical. Unfortunately (well, not so unfortunately), if the inner child isn't taking the center stage of your life, you would most definitely suffer deficiencies and failures in most domains of your life. I'm sure you would like to opt for the former. But hold a sec! There is a clause attached to it!

The inner child is a psychosynthetic experience that spans through all stages of an individual's life. What's the implication of this? Every stage is pivotal in the formation process, and at the same time, every major experience you have at each stage contributes either positively or adversely to your inner child development. This implies that while it is good to have your inner child ageless and active at all times, it is necessary to heal it of negative influence derived from each stage. This, here, is where your duty lies. Reconnecting with your inner child might be a one-time activity if you are careful enough to maintain the connection thereafter, but healing is a rather continuous process because contaminants will keep coming your way! A through healing can only be achieved through a careful inner child work.

The inner child work refers to all efforts and activities put in place to identify, analyze and resolve all hurts and negative emotions buried in the subconscious part of an individual by reason of bad events, traumas, situations, and experiences from their childhood period. It further involves all the processes by which one rediscovers themselves in terms of their true strengths, skills, and traits, all of which were lost to childhood. The process may be carried out individually or with the assistance of a therapist, but the ultimate aim is to reconnect an individual to the joy, confidence, and freedom which they enjoyed as a child in order to relate more meaningfully with life and make the best of it for themselves. Inner child work isn't as difficult as popularized but definitely requires commitment.

Based on this necessity, I provide in this chapter certain tested and trusted healing exercises that have proven useful and efficient for healing the inner child. The recovery process of your inner child is just about to get comprehensive. Come along!

Identify your inner child

The outset of your inner child healing framework is to identify the specific archetype of your inner child. This is necessary to help you tailor your focus and healing process properly. There are about six different inner child archetypes, going by Carl Jung's classification — wounded inner child, orphan inner child, divine inner child, nature inner child, magical inner child, and the eternal inner child archetype. Having identified which particular archetype your inner child belongs, you are now on the right track to individuate your healing.

Reconnect with your inner child

Reestablishing a working relationship with your inner child is the second stage in the all-important process of the inner child healing work. Due to the situations and events revolving around us, we tend to lose connection with the inner child from time to time, or even for a long period of time. This makes a reconnection necessary. If you are wary enough to maintain the connection after one or two reconnections, this would make your inner child healing faster and less exacting. In the previous chapter, I discussed the possible ways to establish a reconnection with your childhood. Ensure you spend ample time with yourself every day, pay more attention to your inner child, focus more on the things that interested you as a child, and more importantly, avoid toxic people!

Communicate with your inner child

Although this exercise is already suggested in the previous one, a separate mention is necessary to emphasize its importance to the healing process of your inner child. Everyone values companionship channeled through constant communication. The same applies to your inner child. It wants to feel loved, safe and supported. If you must maintain a working relationship with him or her, you must communicate openly and steadily. You wonder how? The following simple techniques will be of help:

- ✓ Adopt mantras for yourself. They don't necessarily have to be religious. Any positive statement purposefully directed at your inner child will serve.

✓ Keep a diary. If you love to write, this is a good way of connecting with your inner child. A simple diary of your daily life events will help you divulge all your feelings, hurts and emotions, and at the same time enable you to identify what exactly your inner child prefers in every situation.

✓ Write a letter to your inner child. Letters may not be a daily enterprise, but they wield as much influence as keeping a diary. Write all your childhood desires and interests. This will help to build a bond between you and your inner child.

Take proper note of your inner critic

It is common to override the interests of the inner child while making decisions that pertain to us as adults. You must understand that this is a major way many of us have silenced and suppressed our inner child. Every individual's inner child has a dimension to it that peaks into our consciousness what it prefers or desires in certain situations. Although many scholars see this dimension as a component of conscience, it is much more delicate than the human conscience. It suggests ideas, dictates preferences, requests attention and warns against harm, but more often than not, we decline all of its dictates. To completely recover your inner child, you must pay close attention to what it requests at each point in time. This involves asking questions and checking on it at every point in time.

Undergo a session with a therapist

This is another effective method of healing the inner child, which involves an expert who sees you not as an adult but as a child willing to explore. Regular sessions with your psychotherapist in addition to the other exercises discussed already will assure you that you are in the right step toward recovering your inner child. More so, although you are in the best position to ascertain your inner child needs, experts will assess your progress and make recommendations where necessary.

Adopt the 'play' technique

The 'play' technique is also used very much by expert therapists. You could adopt it in the comfort of your home. Assemble dolls, toy games and all the kiddies' items you used as a child. As awkward as it sounds, this exercise has been found to be one of the most effective because, among other reasons, it is carried out in a relaxed state.

Meditate regularly

This exercise may be used with mantras. Situate yourself in a comfortable environment rid of noises and distractions. Allow your thoughts flow smoothly on their own, and let your mind travel back in time to the sweet times you enjoyed during your childhood. Practice this regularly. It is a simple method that has been found to effectively reconcile adults with their inner child.

The effort to recovering one's inner child is, sure, a demanding one. It requires sheer will, commitment, patience, and enough guidance. Although you can take steps toward achieving this all by yourself, I would recommend that you consult an expert psychotherapist for motivation, guidance, and adequate techniques. Your life is in the best shape when lived as a child's, free from worries and troubles.

WHY INNER CHILD WORK?

Benefits of Healing and Recovering your Inner Child

The most sophisticated people I've ever known had just one thing in common: they were all in touch with their inner children.

Jim Henson

Frustration, distress, unhappiness, failure, relationship problems, career gridlock, phobias, anger, feelings of loneliness, dejection, worthlessness, and depression, among others are apparently not evidence of a good life. In very critical cases, tons of people worldwide have taken their own lives owing to these emotional problems. What many have not discovered, however, is that life would be easier to live, and the world would be a saner clime if we all lived as kids! Imagine the effortlessness, freedom, fun, and whatnot that accompanies childhood. Unfortunately, adulthood stole all that away from us. Well, not totally! We could recover our inner child and all the benefits attached, with the help of inner child work.

Inner child work holds a lot of benefits if well practiced, some of which could be social, mental, or emotional. It is useful for sorting out the multifaceted challenges which confront an adult, most of which stem from the deficiencies incurred from childhood. Such problems include low self-esteem, apathy, excessive self-criticism, self-hatred, depression, anger, pessimism, relationship challenges, numbness, overdependence on others, anxiety, aggression, and so on.

Some of the multidimensional benefits of recovering, healing and reconciling your inner child are:

- You develop a better understanding of yourself, what works for you and what does not.

- You fall in love more with yourself for whom you truly are rather than what you have become or achieved.

- Your self-confidence is boosted sporadically. You can now dare to do more because you understand that it is what your inner child wants.

- You gain a deeper understanding of relationships, and can now separate the toxic ones from the helpful ones.

- You can now access the beautiful memories that were long forgotten.

- Your innate skills are not only revealed, but they are also renewed.

- You feel actively in control of yourself again, and not influenced adversely by external factors.

- Your life takes on an entirely new and meaningful dimension.

- You can now set life goals purposefully and with the right mindset, skills, and abilities to achieve them.

- Living becomes fun again!

The benefits are endless and manifest differently based on individuals. It is physiologically impossible to become kids again, but definitely, we can live like kids again, enjoying the bliss that comes with the age. The approach lies in rediscovering, reawakening and reconciling with the inner child in each of us! According to C.S Lewis, I hope that *'someday, you will be old enough to start reading fairy tales again.'*

ABOUT THE BOOK

Have you heard of the term 'inner child work' but you cannot really weave your mind around it?

Are you facing a problem right now and you have been told that your wounded inner child might just be responsible?

Are you looking for a simple but comprehensive relatable guide for healing your injured inner child?

If you answered yes to any of the above questions, this workbook is written for you! Like you, there is at least one in three persons worldwide whose adult challenges originate from one or more ugly experiences from their childhood experiences which have over time been sedimented into their subconscious mind, thereby affecting their activities and relationships as adults. But then, what precisely is the inner child? How does it wield so much influence on our lives? You ask. Great questions! If you have ever caught yourself making soap bubbles during shower, or giggling without an obvious cause when you are alone, or making vehicle sounds with your mouth, you would understand that your inner child manifests itself, which is a sign that, like every other person alive, you have an inner child willing to be noticed and nurtured.

Although your inner child embodies both good and negative experiences from the past, it is often the case that the positive side to it, which encompasses feelings of love, compassion for others, happiness, positivism, and confidence, among others, are subdued by the negative experiences you experienced while growing. This explains why you need an inner child work.

In this workbook, you will discover:

- Hidden facts about your inner child
- Your specific inner child archetype as classified by Carl Jung
- Signs of an injured inner child
- Lucia Capachionne's therapy for your wounded inner child
- The many benefits of having a healed inner child
- Basic DIY exercises with which you can heal your inner child
- How to break free from the consequences of a dysfunctional family

- Ways to reconnect with your childhood roots of happiness

  ...and lots more!

The Inner Child Healing discusses in six simple relatable chapters the practicable methods of healing your inner child with little or no assistance from an expert. Ideas suggested in this guidebook have not only been tested but have also been psychologically approved for their effectiveness and speedy results. If you are hoping to enjoy all the bliss, freedom and whatnot that comes with childhood again, perfect inner child work is all you need. Imagine a world free of the daily troubles of adult life but full of the happiness of childhood. You too can be part of the world. Unlock your power to heal your inner child today.

Printed in Great Britain
by Amazon